Black Hole

W9-CKL-6

my guide to the solar system

CHERRY LAKE PRESS

Published in the United States of America by Cherry Lake Publishing
Ann Arbor, Michigan
www.cherrylakepublishing.com

Reading Adviser: Beth Walker Gambro, MS, Ed., Reading Consultant, Yorkville, IL
Book Design: Jennifer Wahi
Illustrator: Jeff Bane

Photo Credits: © brightstars/iStock.com, 5; © vchal/Shutterstock.com, 7; © FlashMovie/Shutterstock.com, 9; © gremlin/iStock.com, 11; © Elen11/iStock.com, 13; © Lia Koltyrina/Shutterstock.com, 15; © Vadim Sadovski/Shutterstock.com, 17, 19; © Dima Zel/Shutterstock.com, 21; © Lyu Hu/Shutterstock.com, 23; Cover, 2-3, 6, 16, 22, 24, Jeff Bane

Cherry Lake Press is an imprint of Cherry Lake Publishing Group.

Library of Congress Cataloging-in-Publication Data

Names: Devera, Czeena, author. | Bane, Jeff, 1957- illustrator.
Title: Black hole / by Czeena Devera ; illustrated by Jeff Bane.
Description: Ann Arbor, Michigan : Cherry Lake Publishing, [2022] | Series:
    My guide to the solar system | Audience: Grades K-1 |
Identifiers: LCCN 2021036518 (print) | LCCN 2021036519 (ebook) | ISBN
    9781534199057 (hardcover) | ISBN 9781668900192 (paperback) | ISBN
    9781668901632 (pdf) | ISBN 9781668905951 (ebook)
Subjects: LCSH: Black holes (Astronomy)--Juvenile literature.
Classification: LCC QB843.B55 D48 2023 (print) | LCC QB843.B55 (ebook) |
    DDC 523.8/875--dc23
LC record available at https://lccn.loc.gov/2021036518
LC ebook record available at https://lccn.loc.gov/2021036519

Printed in the United States of America
Corporate Graphics

About the author: Czeena Devera grew up in the red-hot heat of Arizona surrounded by books. Her childhood bedroom had built-in bookshelves that were always full. She now lives in Michigan with an even bigger library of books.

About the illustrator: Jeff Bane and his two business partners own a studio along the American River in Folsom, California, home of the 1849 Gold Rush. When Jeff's not sketching or illustrating for clients, he's either swimming or kayaking in the river to relax.

I'm a black hole. I like to stay mysterious. Not much is known about me.

In fact, I'm invisible. I don't reflect light. But strange things happen around me. This is how **scientists** know that I exist.

I'm formed when a giant star explodes. This is called a **supernova**.

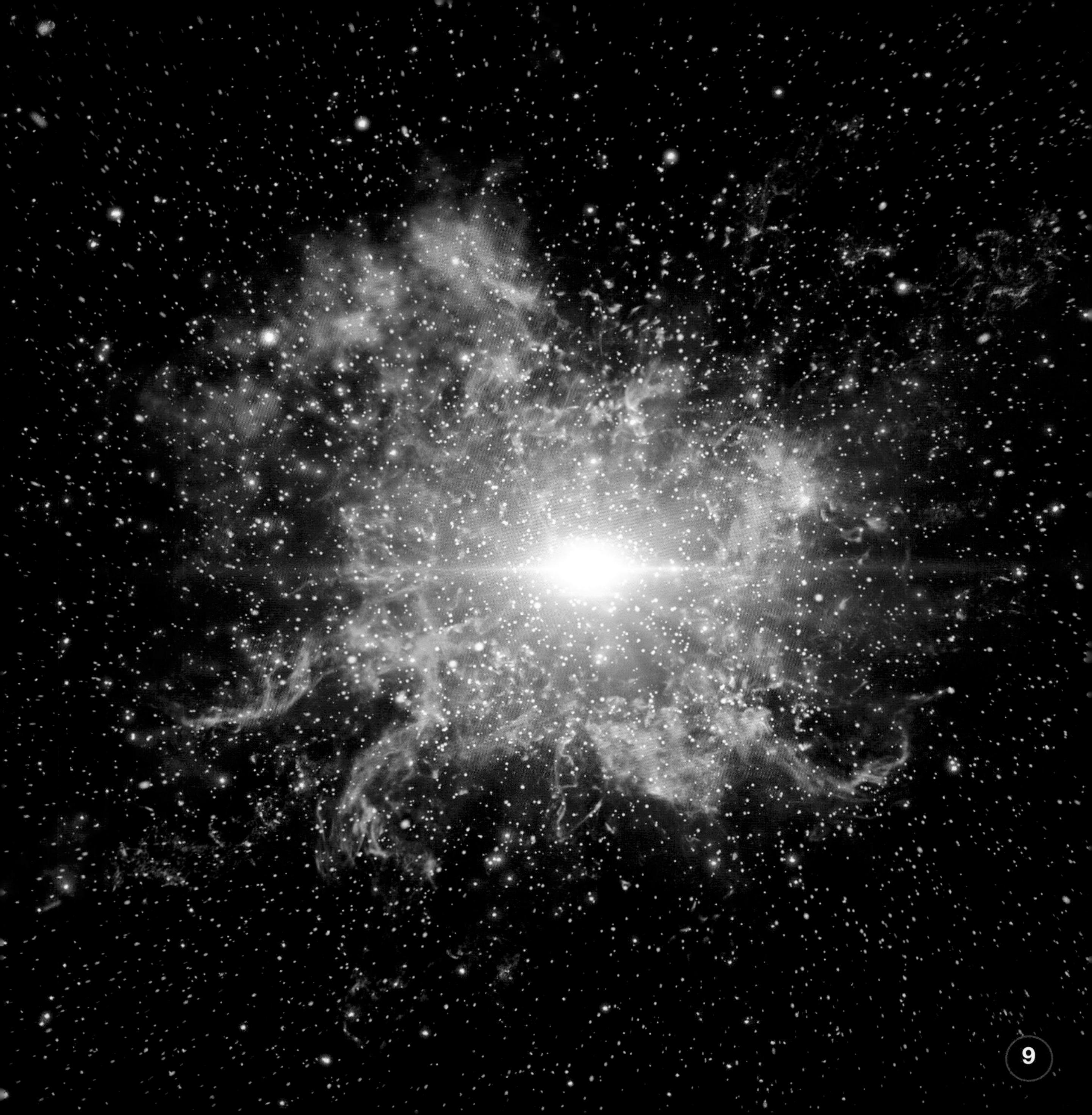

My **gravity** is so strong. Nothing escapes me. Not even light!

Sometimes I can get really big. I pull in everything around me. I can even pull in other stars!

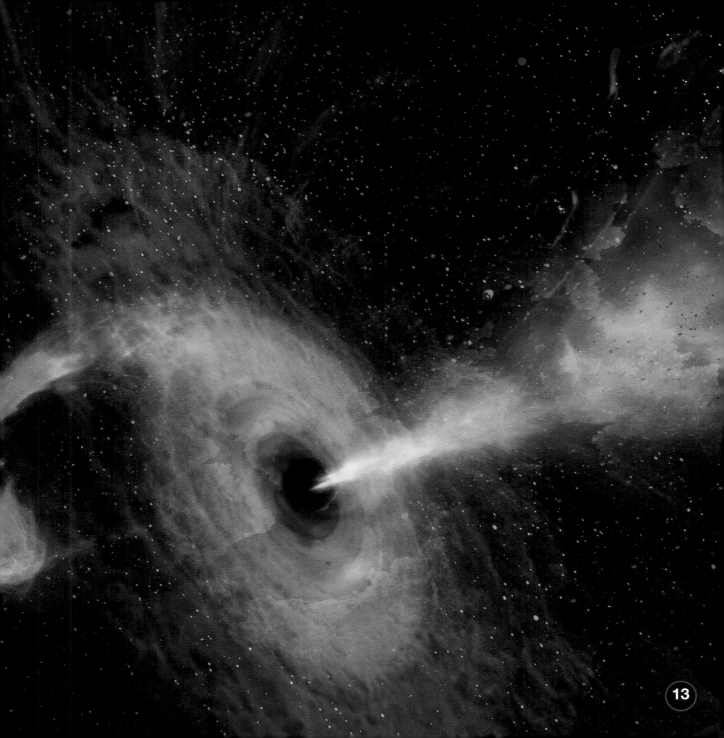

I have a special **boundary** called the event horizon. This is the point where I can pull in things.

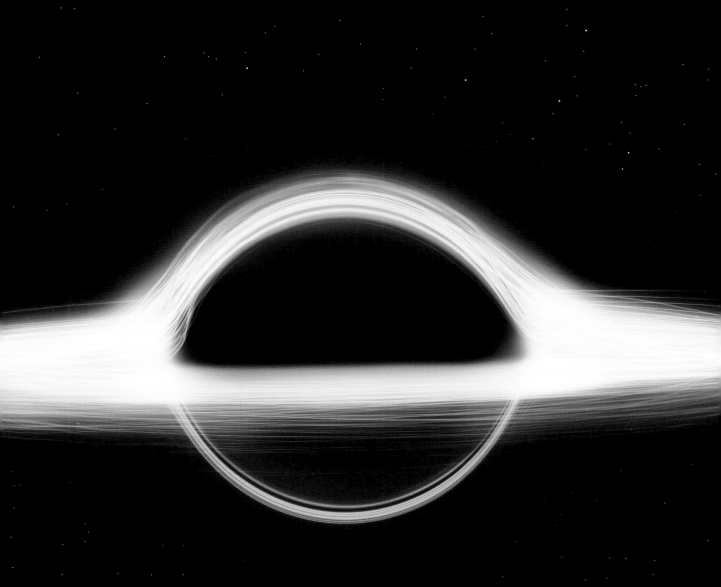

How big is your family?

There are a bunch of us. But we generally come in two sizes. These are stellar mass and supermassive.

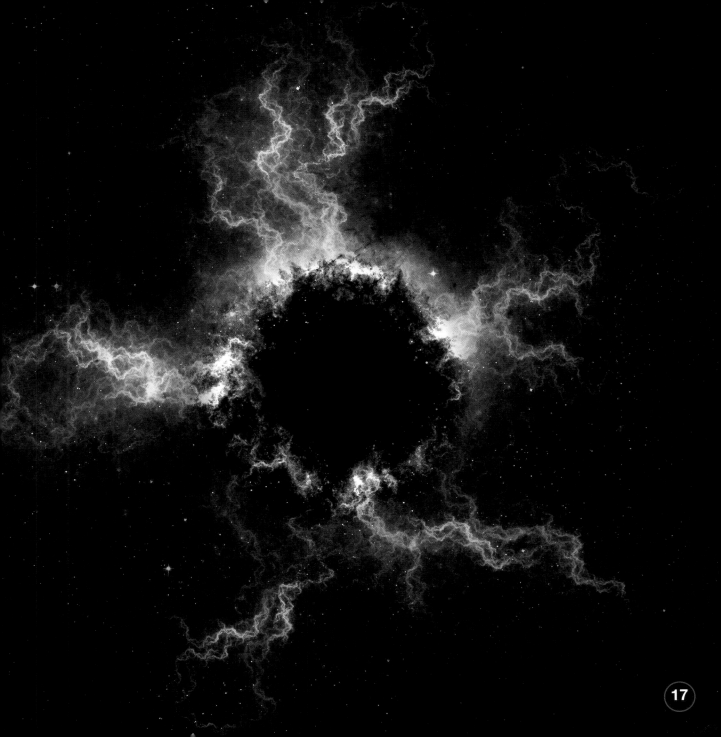

Stellar mass black holes are slightly bigger than the Sun. They're about 10 to 24 times bigger.

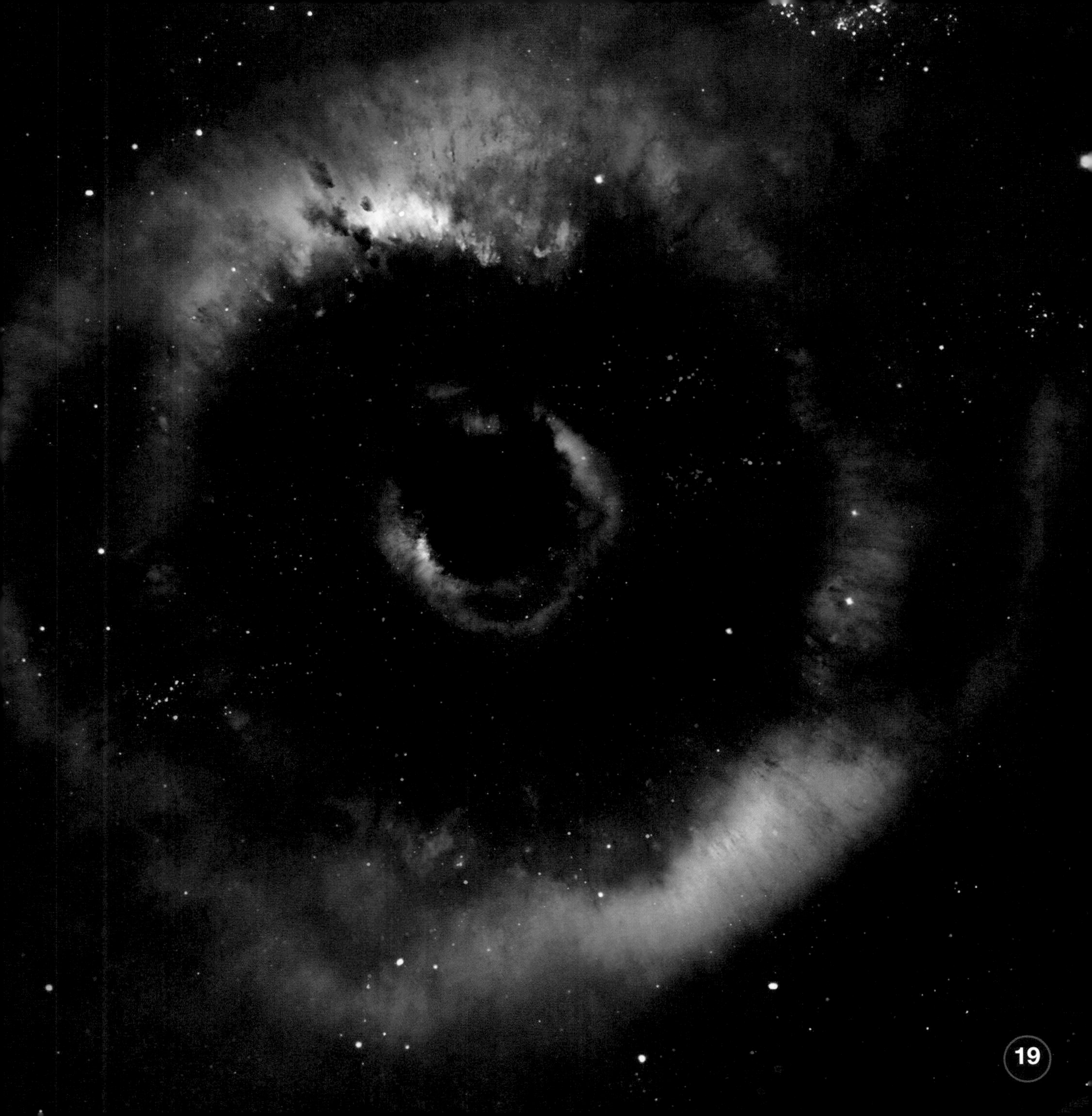

Supermassive black holes are way bigger than the Sun. They're millions or billions times bigger. Scientists believe these black holes are the center of some **galaxies**.